W9-BJN-304

MATH ACADEMY

PLACE VALUE

PRIZE

By Kirsty Holmes

CRABTREE
PUBLISHING COMPANY
WWW.CRABTREEBOOKS.COM

CRABTREE
PUBLISHING COMPANY
WWW.CRABTREEBOOKS.COM

Author:
Kirsty Holmes

Editorial director:
Kathy Middleton

Editors:
William Anthony, Janine Deschenes

Proofreader:
Crystal Sikkens

Graphic design:
Ian McMullen

Prepress technician:
Katherine Berti

Print coordinator:
Katherine Berti

All images are courtesy of Shutterstock.com, unless otherwise specified. With thanks to Getty Images, Thinkstock Photo, and iStockphoto.

Front Cover: New Africa, ShutterStockStudio iunewind, vipman, Nadya_Art

Interior: Background – ngaga, eurobanks. Characters: Maya: Rajesh Narayanan. Zoe: Dave Pot. Robert: Shift Drive. Abdul: Ahmad Ihsan. Professor Tengent: Roman Samborskyi. Cy-Bud: AlesiaKan. 6 – Winai Tepsuttinun, LHF Graphics. 7 – Vivid Pixels, BlackRoader. 8 – Katerina Pereverzeva. 9 – kurhan. 10 – TrifonenkoIvan. 12 – Konstantin Faraktinov. 13 – kurhan, archideaphoto

All facts, statistics, web addresses, and URLs in this book were verified as valid and accurate at time of writing. No responsibility for any changes to external websites or references can be accepted by either the author or publisher.

Library and Archives Canada Cataloguing in Publication

Title: Place value prize / by Kirsty Holmes.
Names: Holmes, Kirsty, author.
Description: Series statement: Math academy | Includes index.
Identifiers: Canadiana (print) 20200394177 |
  Canadiana (ebook) 20200394371 |
  ISBN 9781427130112 (hardcover) |
  ISBN 9781427130150 (softcover) |
  ISBN 9781427130198 (HTML)
Subjects: LCSH: Place value (Mathematics)—Juvenile literature.
Classification: LCC QA141.3 .H65 2021 | DDC j513.2—dc23

Library of Congress Cataloging-in-Publication Data

Available at the Library of Congress

Crabtree Publishing Company

www.crabtreebooks.com   1–800–387–7650

Published by Crabtree Publishing Company in 2021
© 2020 BookLife Publishing Ltd.

Printed in the U.S.A./022021/CG20201123

Published in Canada
Crabtree Publishing
616 Welland Ave.
St. Catharines, Ontario
L2M 5V6

Published in the United States
Crabtree Publishing
347 Fifth Ave
Suite 1402-145
New York, NY 10016

CONTENTS

Words that are bold, like **this**, can be found in the glossary on page 24.

ATTENDANCE

Another day at Math Academy has begun. Time to take attendance! Meet some students in class 301.

Maya
Favorite subject:
Place value

Zoë
Favorite subject:
Counting in groups

Professor Tangent

Ali
Favorite subject:
Addition

Robert
Favorite subject:
Subtraction

Today's lesson is all about **place value**. The students will learn answers to these questions.

- What is place value?
- What are ones, tens, and hundreds?
- How do **charts** and **cubes** help us understand place value?

Math Academy is a school especially for kids who love math and solving problems.

Do I hear the bell?

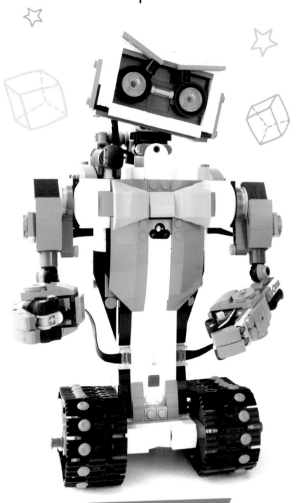

Cy-Bud
Favorite subject:
Facts and figures

MORNING LESSON

Last week, class 301 won the school mathletics competition. Their prize arrives today, and they are all very excited.

I'm so proud of you, my little mathletes!

Congratulations Class 301!

#1

YOU ARE THE WINNERS!

YOUR PRIZE: A TRUCKLOAD OF CUBES!

Suddenly, a truck pulled in front of the school. The students rushed outside. The truck was completely full of cubes!

I didn't know we would get a REAL truckload!

LUNCHTIME

The children can't wait to use the new cubes. The students will use the cubes to add, subtract, and make groups.

There are so many cubes! They will help us improve our math skills.

The class now has the task of **counting** how many cubes they have. The school janitor, Mr. Fraction, brings all the boxes from the truck to the classroom.

Here are the boxes, Professor Tangent. Enjoy your prize, children!

The class opens the first box. One at a time, they take cubes from the box and start to count. To count, they start with one, then name the numbers in order.

The single cubes are **ones**.

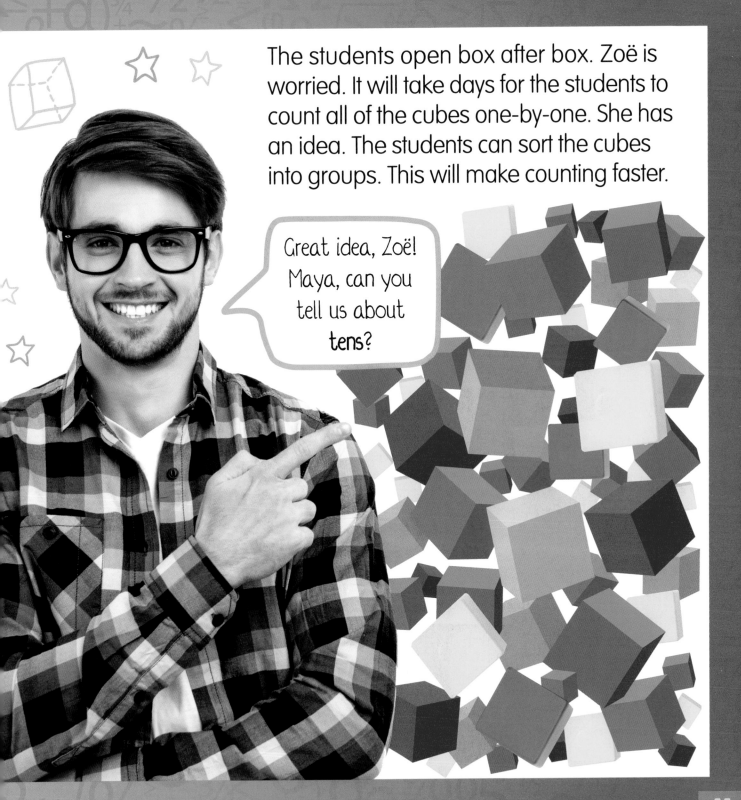

The students open box after box. Zoë is worried. It will take days for the students to count all of the cubes one-by-one. She has an idea. The students can sort the cubes into groups. This will make counting faster.

Great idea, Zoë! Maya, can you tell us about **tens**?

MAYA MAKES IT WORK

Maya explains that ten is a **bundle** of ten ones. The students can sort the cubes into bundles of ten. Then, they can count the groups by ten.

Counting by ten is much faster than counting by one.

The students sort nine groups of ten.
Starting at 10, they count by ten up to 90.
Counting is much quicker this way!

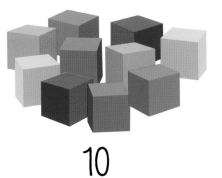

10

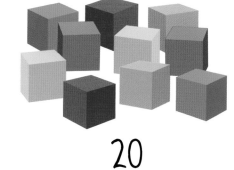

20

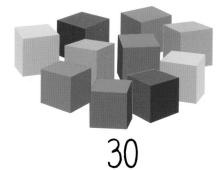

30

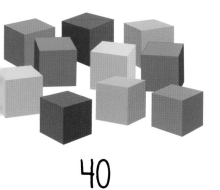

40

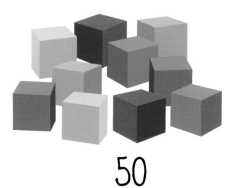

50

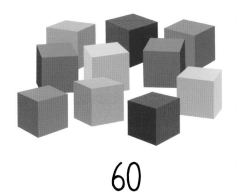

60

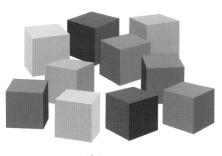

70

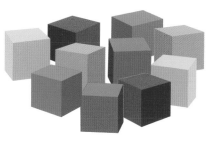

80

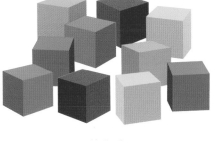

90

It isn't long before Ali spots more boxes hidden behind Professor Tangent's desk. Maya jumps up. She explains that the students can sort the cubes into bigger groups.

We can make a bundle of ten tens. This makes one hundred!

10

20

30

40

50

60

70

80

90

100

Each number from 11 to 19 has one bundle
of ten with ones left over. Each number from
110 to 199 has one bundle of one hundred
with tens, and sometimes ones, left over.

The number 17 is one
bundle of ten and
seven ones left over.

The number 62 is six bundles
of ten and two ones left over.

The number 120 is one bundle
of 100 and two bundles of ten.

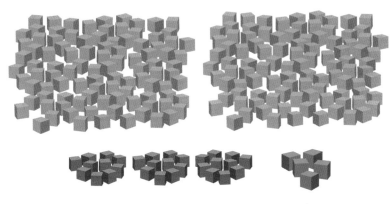

The number 235 is two bundles
of one hundred, three bundles
of ten, and five ones left over.

MAKE IT RIGHT WITH MATH

The students look at all of the cubes. They are now sorted into many groups of hundreds, tens, and ones. It is time to count by ones, tens, and hundreds to find out how many cubes they have. Understanding place value will help them find the **total** number!

First, we should count the ones. These are the cubes left over that did not make a bundle of ten. Can you count the cubes I am holding?

The students count three ones. Next, it is time to count the tens, or each group of ten.

How many groups of ten do you see?

The students count seven tens. Finally, they need to count the hundreds, or each group of one hundred.

How many hundreds do you see?

The students count two hundreds. They have counted all the cubes! Maya uses a chart to write down the total number of cubes. The chart shows how each **digit** has a different place value: one, ten, and one hundred!

We have 273 cubes! Wow!

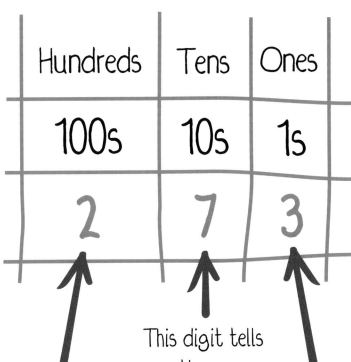

Hundreds	Tens	Ones
100s	10s	1s
2	7	3

This digit tells us there are two groups of one hundred. Its place value is 200.

This digit tells us there are seven groups of ten. Its place value is 70.

This digit tells us there are three ones. Its place value is 3.

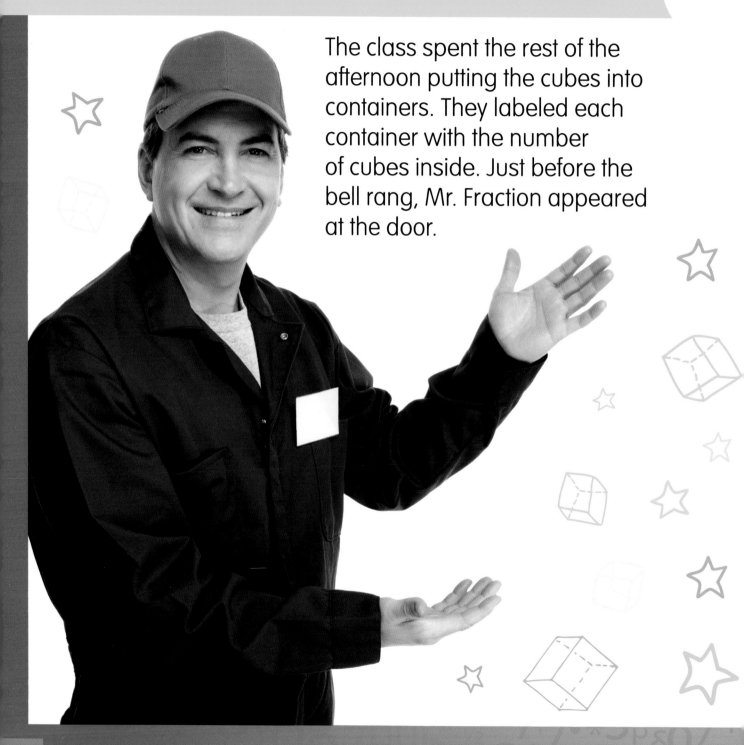

The class spent the rest of the afternoon putting the cubes into containers. They labeled each container with the number of cubes inside. Just before the bell rang, Mr. Fraction appeared at the door.

Another truck has pulled into the parking lot...and it's full of cubes, too!

Where will we put all of these cubes?

The students in class 301 learned that cubes can represent, or stand for, numbers. The chart below shows cubes that represent groups of one, ten, and one hundred.

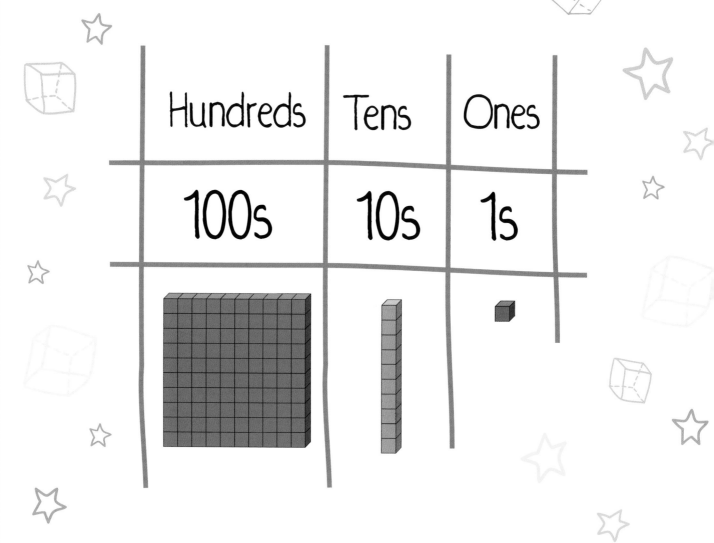

Hundreds	Tens	Ones
100s	10s	1s

Can you find the numbers represented by these cubes?
Use the chart on page 22 to help you.

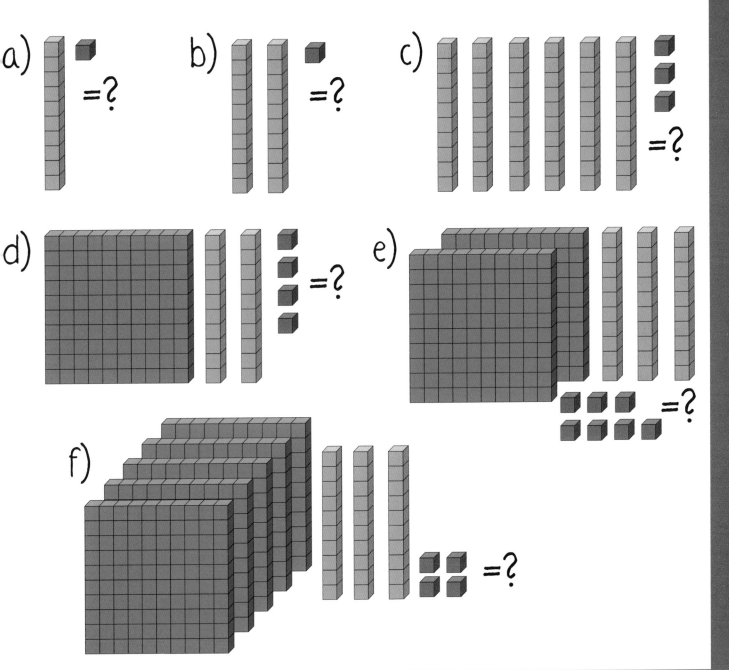

a) =?

b) =?

c) =?

d) =?

e) =?

f) =?

GLOSSARY

BUNDLE — Objects put together in a group, such as tens

CHARTS — Information in the form of a table

COUNTING — To say numbers in order, starting with one

CUBES — Objects that have six square sides

DIGIT — A written symbol for any of the numbers zero to nine

ONES — Number for single objects or units

PLACE VALUE — The value of a digit based on its position in a number

TENS — Groups of ten ones

TOTAL — A final number reached by adding other numbers together

INDEX